Venus

Earth

Asteroid Belt

Saturn

Neptune

A Look at Comets

A Look at Comets

Comets

Ray Spangenburg and Kit Moser

Franklin Watts

A DIVISION OF SCHOLASTIC INC.
NEW YORK · TORONTO · LONDON · AUCKLAND
SYDNEY · MEXICO CITY · NEW DELHI · HONG KONG
DANBURY, CONNECTICUT

In memory of
MENCK
whose love of life
is sorely missed

The photograph on the cover shows an image of Comet vor blauen over the horizon. The photograph opposite the title page shows people viewing a comet in the night sky.

Library of Congress Cataloging-in-Publication Data
    Spangenburg, Ray, 1939–
    A look at comets / Ray Spangenburg and Kit Moser.
    p. cm.—(Out of this world)
Summary: A comprehensive look at comets, from man's earliest observations of "hairy stars," to recent sightings of Comet Shoemaker-Levy 9 and Hale-Bopp, to future space missions to study comets in the outer solar system.
Includes bibliographical references and index.
    ISBN 0-531-11926-2 (lib. bdg.)   0-531-16686-4 (pbk.)
    1. Comets—Juvenile literature. [1. Comets.] I. Moser, Diane, 1944–
II. Title. III. Out of this world (Franklin Watts, Inc.)
523.6—dc21   2003005808

Acknowledgments

To all those who have contributed to *A Look at Comets,* we would like to take this opportunity to say "thank you," with special appreciation to our editors on this project, Melissa Palestro, who has shown both great patience and courage, and Christine Florie, who saw it through with both grit and grace. We would also like to give credit to Melissa Stewart, whose originality and vision provided the initial sparks for this series. Additionally, we would like to thank Margaret Carruthers, planetary geologist, Washington, DC, and Dr. Richard Ash (University of Maryland), who reviewed the manuscript and provided many insightful suggestions. If any inaccuracies remain, the fault is ours, not theirs. Finally, many thanks to Tony Reichhardt and John Rhea, our editors at the former *Space World Magazine,* who first started us out on these fascinating journeys into the regions of space, space science, and technology.

Contents

Comet 81 as observed from Cerro Paranal, Chile

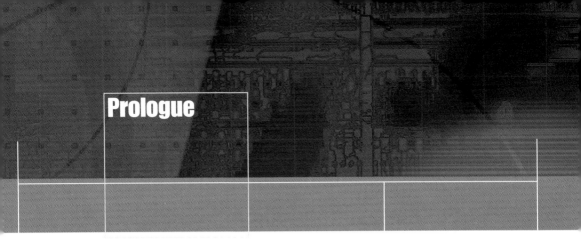

Comets
as Clues

Comets are exciting and they can seem mysterious. A comet can seem to appear out of nowhere—a bright, new object in the skies. Night after night it is there, moving steadily against the background of stars. As it approaches the Sun, it glows brighter and grows a vast tail. The tail may be bushy and broad. It may spread out far behind the glow of the comet. The comet makes its way toward the Sun, circles around our solar system's star, and then makes its way back. Now, the tail spreads out in front of the comet. Slowly the tail and the comet grow dimmer. Then, one day the comet and its tail have both disappeared from view.

To scientists, comets have always been fascinating—the source of many mysteries to be solved. Where do comets come from? Where do they go when they leave Earth's neighborhood? What are they made of? Why do they seem to travel in and out of the solar system on paths so different from the planets, moons, and asteroids?

Comets are some of the oldest, most primitive objects in the solar system. They are relics from the time of the solar system's first formation. They are made of the same elements as the early solar nebula from which everything in the solar system—Sun, planets, moons, and asteroids—took form. However, because comets have hardly changed at all in the 4.5 billion years since that time, scientists consider them primitive compared with many other objects, such as Earth, which have continually changed and evolved.

Recently, scientists have discovered exciting new facts about comets—facts that make them more intriguing than ever. They have found out that comets carry onboard significant amounts of water ice and dust made of carbon-based compounds—some of the most important ingredients of life. Some scientists think these ingredients may have traveled to Earth, during a period over 4 billion years ago, when objects in the solar system were not stable and settled into their orbits as they are now. Planets, moons, comets, and asteroids all received heavy bombardment, smacked by chunks of rock ranging from microscopic to the size of a city and bigger. Earth has received its share of impacts—and comets played an important role in those impacts. Comets, which formed in the coldest regions of the solar system, retained some of the substances easily lost to heat, such as water ice and carbon monoxide and carbon dioxide ice. So, when comets hit Earth, they may have brought important loads of water ice and carbon-based compounds at a moment when conditions were just right for the very beginnings of life.

Today, scientists study comets because they are like time machines—they take us back, far back, to another time when there were no humans to take pictures or record the moment. They offer a glimpse into the past when the solar system was still very young and life on Earth had not yet begun.

This British illuminated manuscript from the fourteenth century uses the image of a man observing a comet as an illustration for the letter "C."

Chapter 1

Comet
Tales

The first people to notice the unusual movement of a comet and its blaze in the nighttime skies lived thousands of years ago. Ancient observers watched the heavens with great interest. As they looked skyward, the majestic expanse of stars seemed to move from horizon to horizon in a nightly journey. They watched as long ago as the time of the ancient Chaldeans (about 2000 B.C.E.) and the Babylonians (about 1900 B.C.E.)—and no doubt earlier, before records were kept. These early astronomers noticed that the stars seemed to move in regular patterns throughout the year. Observing these movements, they began to record the patterns. They called these patterns the zodiac, including the entire parade of star groups now known as constellations, or groups of stars. By connecting the dots of light in their minds, the ancients

The ancient Babylonians were famous for their astronomical observations.

saw shapes in the constellations. These shapes reminded them of animals, gods, and heroes. So the stargazers gave them names. Most cultures saw stories in the starry skies. Different cultures included different stars in these groups and gave them various names. Most

This stained-glass window depicts the signs of the zodiac. Astrology is based on the belief that celestial bodies can affect everything from individual personality and behavior to the course of human events.

people today are familiar with the starred belt of Orion, the throne of Cassiopeia, and the Big Dipper. These names come primarily from Greek and Roman skywatchers.

Against the backdrop of these stars, ancient astronomers noticed five oddly moving lights they called the "planets," from the Greek word for "wanderers." These specks did not twinkle as the stars did, and they did not seem to travel with the stars. Instead they cut their own paths across the skies. They are known today as Mercury, Venus, Mars, Jupiter, and Saturn. The ancients also noticed certain infrequent visitors to the skies they watched so carefully. These glowing bodies appeared, it seemed, from nowhere. Night after night, they moved slowly across the sky toward the Sun. A blazing tail trailed out, away from the Sun, and they sometimes showed alarming changes in brightness. Many ancient observers believed these apparitions were omens of extreme danger to come.

Among the early astronomers, the most detailed records come from observers in China. Among the earliest is a record from the eleventh century B.C.E. (possibly about 1059 B.C.E.), when astronomers in China recorded a comet with a bushy tail that pointed east. The comet appeared about the time King Wu-Wang went to war against King Chou, and a connection was thought to exist between the two events. In China at that time, astronomers were also astrologers, often employed by kings to predict the future. (Sometimes people confuse astronomy and astrology—and, in fact, in ancient times the distinction was fuzzy. However, today's astronomers study the nature of the universe and its objects through observation and

William Shakespeare was just one of many great writers who in their work used the appearance of a comet as an omen. "When beggars die, there are no comets seen," Shakespeare wrote. "The heavens themselves blaze forth the death of princes." This is the renowned nineteenth-century French painter Eugene Delacroix's illustration of one of the opening scenes from Shakespeare's play *Hamlet*.

experiment. The purpose of astrology, by contrast, is to predict future events, warn of future disasters, and provide advice, based on a nonscientific belief that the positions of stars and planets influence events and conditions on Earth.) Comets turned up at odd times and seemed to have a connection with

CAP.° 63.°

trouble. It is often difficult to tell the difference between *coincidence* (when two events occur at the same time but have no cause-and-effect connection) and *causation* (when one event is the cause or trigger of another). So, for centuries the astronomers/astrologers in China thought of comets as important signs of trouble to come. In 1973 a book of silk pages dating back to 168 B.C.E. was discovered in an ancient tomb at Mawangdui, China. The book contained many drawings of natural phenomena, such as clouds, rainbows, and the Moon. It also included 29 illustrations of comets, showing some 27 different types. This discovery helps show how important comets were and how carefully astronomers had observed them.

Egyptian astronomers called them "hairy stars" because the long tail extending from the body of the comet looked like a long trail of flowing hair. The name was handed down, and that is why we call these objects

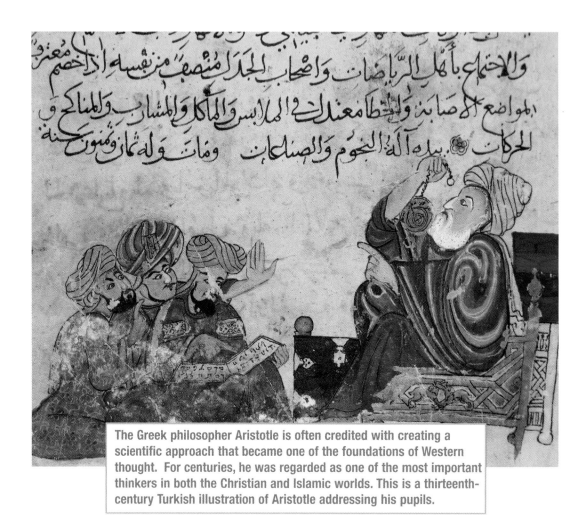

وَالِاجْتِمَاعِ بِأَهْلِ الرِّيَاضَاتِ وَأَصْحَابِ الْجَدَلِ مُنْصَبٌّ مِنْ نَفْسِهِ إِذَا خُصِمُوا
الْمَوَاضِعَ الْأَصَابِيَةَ وَالِاخْتِطَا مَعَنْدَكُ وَالْمَلَابِسِ وَالْمَأْكَلِ وَالْمَشَارِبِ وَالْمَنَاكِحِ وَ
الْحَرَكَاتِ ﷽ بِدِهِ آلَةَ النُّجُومِ وَالصِّنَاعَاتِ وَمَاتَ وَلَهُ ثَمَانٍ وَثَمَانُونَ سَنَةً

The Greek philosopher Aristotle is often credited with creating a scientific approach that became one of the foundations of Western thought. For centuries, he was regarded as one of the most important thinkers in both the Christian and Islamic worlds. This is a thirteenth-century Turkish illustration of Aristotle addressing his pupils.

"comets," based on the Greek word *kometes* meaning long-haired. Greek skywatchers thought comets were messengers from the gods. Romans believed they foretold some evil to come. Every culture noticed comets, and stories about them sprang up.

Any attempt at understanding comets was made more difficult when the great Greek scientist-philosopher Aristotle

(384–322 B.C.E.) made a big mistake in the fourth century B.C.E. He based his entire view of the universe on the idea that Earth was at the center of everything. Because his influence was powerful, scientists tried for centuries to make the facts they observed fit the great philosopher's mistaken idea.

Working with this geocentric (Earth-centered) view, people could not figure out how comets fit into this system. How could they be traveling between the planets? They did not seem to travel around Earth the way Aristotle thought everything else did. So, Aristotle resolved the problem for the moment by saying that comets occur within Earth's atmosphere. This view of comets contributed enormously to the idea that comets showed up when something bad was about to happen on Earth. It was easy to imagine a connection between the sudden appearance of a comet and events taking place on Earth, such as earthquakes or volcanoes erupting. So wars and suicides and illnesses also might be caused by comets. Even if months went by without any catastrophes, eventually something would happen that the comet must have been warning about.

Centuries later, a Greek astronomer named Ptolemy (ca. 100–170 C.E.) made observations in Alexandria, Egypt. To make Aristotle's theory fit his observations and studies of the planets and stars that others had made, Ptolemy made some complicated adjustments to the theory that allowed him and most of the rest of the scientific community to hang on to the geocentric idea. So, the idea that Earth was at the center of everything lasted for another 1,500 years!

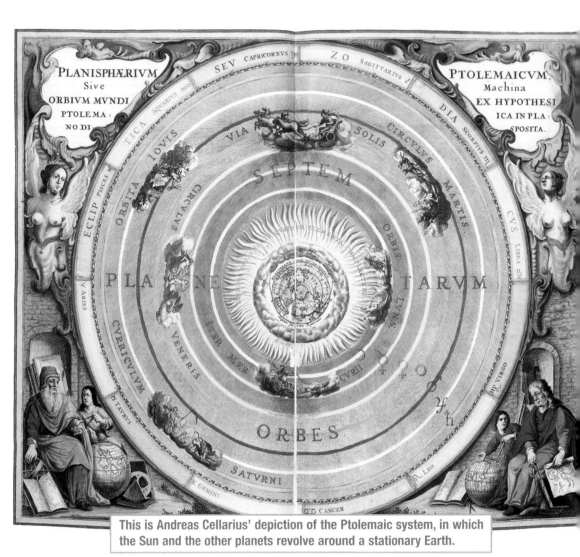

This is Andreas Cellarius' depiction of the Ptolemaic system, in which the Sun and the other planets revolve around a stationary Earth.

No one succeeded in challenging the Earth-centered, or geocentric, view of the universe until a Polish mathematician named Nicolaus Copernicus (1473–1543) showed by his calculations that the theory simply did not fit the facts reported by observers. He showed that the Sun is at the center of the system and all the planets, including Earth, revolve around it—the sun-centered, or heliocentric view. That change laid the groundwork for establishing some new, more scientific ideas about comets, what they were, how they moved, where they traveled, and where they came from.

Meteor Showers

Sometimes, the sky lights up with hundreds—even hundreds of thousands—of showering lights, known as *meteor showers*. When you look at the sky during a meteor shower, all the meteors seem to be coming from the same point—a region of the sky astronomers call the *radiant point*. For reference, astronomers name the showers after the star or constellation that seems to be closest to the radiant point.

Long ago, astronomers noticed that these big meteor showers seemed to occur on regular schedules. Even more confusing— not all schedules were yearly. Some occurred at much longer intervals, often several years apart. So, what is the connection between comets and meteors? As it turns out, meteor showers occur when Earth passes through the trail of a comet. As a comet approaches the Sun, the heat vaporizes the ice. Particles of dust and chunks of rock become broken off from the cracks and fissures that form. A comet may have many craters and jagged edges where chunks have broken off. These chunks and particles of dust lag behind, following along in the comet's orbit—and if the comet crosses Earth's orbit, some of those clumps of material

Not all superstitions and fears about comets belong to the distant past. On March 26, 1997, the dead bodies of 39 members of a small cult called "Heaven's Gate" were discovered in their mansion in Rancho Santa Fe in Southern California. At first, no one could understand what had happened. Finally, investigators revealed that the Heaven's Gate cult held a strange—and deadly—belief about a comet named Hale-Bopp, which was currently appearing in the nighttime skies. As the story unfolded, the roles of rumor and "harmless sensationalism" became clear.

To most people, Hale-Bopp was just another comet, discovered independently by amateur astronomers Alan Hale and Thomas Bopp on July 23, 1995. However, most of the rest of the world paid little attention as they went about their daily business.

The Hale-Bopp story took a bizarre turn, though, in November of 1996, when an amateur astronomer called in to the "Art Bell Show," a popular national talk-radio program. The caller told Bell that he had photographed a large object immediately behind the comet. He said it was perhaps as big as four Earths. The Bell Show specialized in extreme fringe topics often dealing with the occult and pseudoscientific. It had a large audience and the story of Hale-Bopp and its "mysterious companion" soon began to spread. In the next few weeks other callers claimed they had also seen the object behind the comet and one even sent Bell a "photo."

Astronomers explained that the so-called companion in the photo was merely a distant normal star seen through the comet's tail. The story and rumors, though, refused to go away. Soon people began to describe the so-called Hale-Bopp "companion" as the "UFO" flying behind Hale-Bopp.

It was inevitable that the stories would come to the attention of the small California cult that operated a Web page called "Heaven's Gate." One of many such cults throughout history, the members of Heaven's Gate believed that the world would soon end. They also believed, as most cults do, that they would be saved to live a new existence in a higher and better place.

that got left behind wind up right in Earth's path. So, as Earth travels around the Sun, it may encounter many micrometeoroids for several years following the comet's visit. Since the material may remain floating in the same part of Earth's orbit for a long

Writing on their Web page, the cult declared, "Hale-Bopp's approach is the 'marker' we've been waiting for—the time for the arrival of the spacecraft from the Level Above Human to take us home to 'Their World'—in the literal Heavens."

Sometime during the few days preceding the discovery of their bodies, members of the cult had quietly begun to take their own lives.

Hale-Bopp came and went. No spacecraft ever came and the world did not end. Science added to its store of knowledge about the wonders of comets and the general public was treated to another view of their natural beauty.

For the members of Heaven's Gate, though, all life had ended, robbed from them by the terrible powers of rumor, superstition, and ignorance.

time, the Earth encounters this cometary trail at the same time of year, when the same constellation is in view. So, that's why we have patterns of annual meteor showers—a pleasant reminder of a comet that passed by.

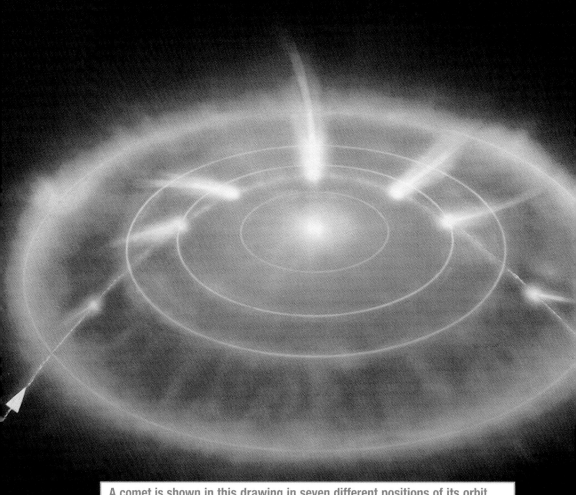

A comet is shown in this drawing in seven different positions of its orbit. Changes in its tail are shaped by the solar wind as it travels around the Sun.

Chapter 2

Uncommon Visitors

Anatomy of a Comet

Since ancient times, two characteristics of a comet were obvious—a roundish, bright object that most observers thought of as the head, and its long, often very bright tail. As astronomers began to use more sophisticated instruments and to see close-up images and data, they realized that comets were more complex than anyone had previously thought.

Scientists have now seen, from visits by spacecraft and observations using improved instruments, that the nucleus of a comet is very small, dark, and irregular in shape. In fact it is so small and dark it often cannot be seen, even by a telescope. Usually, it is only about 0.5 to 12 miles (1 to 20 km) in diameter—tiny and solid. Many astronomers like to describe comets as "dirty snowballs," or "dirty icebergs" because they are rocky and solid, but patches of ice and dirt permeate them—and over half of the nucleus is made of ice. These dirty regions of ice are the source of water vapor and dust that spew from the comet's surface, creating the bright *coma* and spectacular tail.

The bright glow surrounding the nucleus is the coma—a brilliant, luminous gas that appears as the comet nears the orbit of Jupiter. The coma is created by outgassing—that is, gases heated by the Sun boil off the surface of the nucleus. The gases also carry quantities of dust particles along for the ride. Comets rotate, so the dust and gas tend to spiral away from the surface and fan out. This thin halo of gas and dust hovers directly around the nucleus and can extend outward as a vast sphere of atmospheric gas that glows in the sunlight. The glow is caused partly by reflected light on the dust particles and partly because the gas in the coma absorbs ultraviolet radiation and begins to fluoresce like a fluorescent lightbulb. As the comet approaches the Sun, the fluorescence outshines the reflected light.

The coma is the bright, fuzzy ball we see when we look at the head of a comet from Earth. In the case of Halley, this bright sphere is about the size of Jupiter—large enough to hold more than 1,400 Earths! Halley's nucleus is not visible at all during this period—it is hidden beneath the brightness of the coma, which generally grows even brighter as the comet approaches the Sun.

The gas and dust tails of Comet Hale-Bopp are clearly evident in this 1995 photo. A comet's tails may be millions of miles in length.

As the comet absorbs ultraviolet light from the Sun, chemical processes also release hydrogen from the comet. Hydrogen is a very light gas and it easily escapes from the comet's surface and forms an envelope around the comet nucleus. This hydrogen envelope cannot be seen from Earth, but spacecraft have detected it.

No one viewing comets from Earth, however, required rocket science to spot the spectacular, luminous tails that comets usually develop as they come close to the Sun. A comet's tail can be long enough to reach from one planet's orbit to another! Typically, the comet's tail stretches out for millions of miles, as far as the distance from Earth to Mars. Most comets have two tails: a dust tail and an ion, or plasma, tail (composed of uncombined positive ions and electrons). Both the dust tail and the ion tail are created when the force of the solar wind (hydrogen ions speeding away from the Sun) and the pressure of the Sun's radiation sweeps particles outward, away from the Sun. However, different particles are carried at different speeds, according to their mass, size, and charge.

For this reason, the more massive dust tail usually curves, accelerating slowly. Its luminescent glow is caused by reflected sunlight on the tiny surfaces of dust particles. Yet the dust is very sparsely distributed—all the material of a comet's tail could be packed in a single backpack! In most cases the ion tail is carried straight away from the comet and away from the Sun because the ions are lighter and accelerate rapidly. Typically, the ion tail looks thinner and sparser, is blue, and is less reflective than the bright dust tail. Later, as the comet travels back away from the Sun, toward the edge of the solar system, its tail actually extends out in front of it, carried by the solar wind. A second dust tail also may follow the comet, flying, not away from the Sun, but behind the comet.

Not all comets have such showy tails, though. Two comets that don't have much of a tail are Chiron (known as a "dead" comet) and Schwassmann-Wachmann 1 (with an orbit near Jupiter). Instead, they have only a coma and short, faint tails

Astrophysicists—physicists who study the structure of the universe—have found that all stars, including the Sun, formed from molecular clouds called *solar nebulae* (the plural for the Latin word *nebula*, which means "cloud"). Some 4.56 billion years ago, in a dense region of such a cloud, our Sun began to form. First, the cloud began to grow denser as its gravity attracted surrounding material toward its dense core. As atoms fell ever faster toward the core, they bumped into each other, causing friction, and the temperature rose. A protostar—the beginning of a star—began to form as more and more material fell into the core, which shrank as it became denser and denser. As the infant star became hotter, it stopped shrinking and a process called nuclear fusion began to take place—the same process that powers a hydrogen bomb. Atoms of hydrogen, of which these clouds of gas are primarily composed, began to combine to form helium, and in the process, they gave off enormous energy.

Meanwhile, the increasing gravity of the Sun's growing mass continued to attract more and more gas and dust from the surrounding interstellar regions. This was the beginning of the solar system. As the Sun continued to form, the leftover dust and gas began to clump into smaller, dense clouds traveling in orbit around the newborn star. As these clumps—called *planetesimals*—traveled, they swept up more and more material out of the surrounding areas. The more material the planetesimals gathered up, the bigger they got and the greater their gravitational pull. The particles of these large clumps coalesced, or united, to become the planets of our solar system. Smaller clumps became the moons of planets. And still smaller clumps were not big enough to attract a lot more gas and dust. They couldn't sweep material out of the surrounding area the way the larger planets did. So, some got kicked out of the solar system. Some collided with planets and broke up or else combined with planets. Some were captured into a planet's orbit as small moons. Some were broken up into fragments by *tidal forces.*

Finally, some are still out there, preserved intact, orbiting in space, and because they are unchanged, they are known as the oldest, most primitive objects in the solar system. These objects became asteroids, meteoroids, and comets. Of these, the comets are small, dark, incredibly cold objects caught at the outermost edge of the solar system, where scientists believe that many still remain. However, occasionally one is hurled toward the Sun—provoked into making the long, lonely voyage to the inner solar system, forced out of the solar system's deep freeze by the influence of a passing star or other disturbance in this otherwise dark, silent region known as the Oort Cloud.

On a clear dark night you don't need a telescope or binoculars to see that the sky is filled with wondrous sights. In the late eighteenth century, Charles Messier spent a lot of nights looking up at the dark skies through his telescope.

This photograph illustrates the so-called nebula effect. A nebula is an interstellar cloud of gas or dust; its presence can affect the apparent color of a star's light.

Messier was a French astronomer whose love in life was looking for new comets. All those bright objects in the sky didn't make his life any easier. Since it was comets he was looking for, the trick was to separate the wheat from the chaff, or the comets from everything else. The single stars were easy to sort out, but the skies were also cluttered up with all kinds of other obscure objects known as star clusters and nebulae. These distant cloudlike masses of stars and hazy masses of dust, particles, and gases could take up valuable viewing time on a comet search. When Messier saw a fuzzy, cometlike object in his viewer, he had to ask himself, Was it a new comet that was being discovered, or just another nebula? The only way to know was to keep checking on it, studying its apparent movements in the sky. If it behaved more like a nebula than a comet—that is, it remained relatively fixed in the sky, like the stars—he would have to discard it and move on.

What he needed, Messier decided, was a list of all those non-comet objects, and he decided to compile just such a record. He would give each nebula or star cluster

because their orbits are entirely within the outer solar system—having what is known as a "short period"—so, even during their "eruptive" times, they are too far from the Sun and also, much of the gassy and dusty material may already have been spent.

a number and note its location in a catalog. Then comet hunters could quickly check it to see if what they were viewing was a possible new comet or an already known and cataloged nebula.

Messier started his catalog in 1760. The job was a long and painstaking one. By 1771 he had put together a preliminary list of 45 nebulae and galaxies and given each a catalog number preceded by M (for Messier). That was the first edition of *Messier's Nebulae and Star Clusters*, better known now as "Messier's Catalog." By 1784, in the second edition of the catalog, his list had reached 103 numbered objects. Later, other astronomers would add to Messier's catalog, which is still useful to astronomers, both professional and amateur, as they view such well-known objects as M1 (the Crab Nebula), M31 (Andromeda), M42 (the Orion Nebula), and M45 (the Pleiades).

Putting his famous catalog together, though, never distracted Messier from his first love, the search for new comets. During his nightly searches, Messier, the "Comet Ferret" (as King Louis XV of France liked to call him), discovered 20 new comets.

This digital image of the Crab Nebula was taken from a telescope on Maui, one of the Hawaiian Islands. This particular nebula is the remnants of a supernova explosion in 1054 that was observed by Chinese astronomers for 23 days. On several occasions it has been mistaken for the appearance of Halley's Comet.

The Beginnings of Cometary Physics

In the days of the early astronomers, though, comets were even more mysterious. However, scientists steadily built new understanding of these uncommon visitors. The shift from a geocentric to heliocentric solar system was a clue to the real nature and location of comets, but not the only one. Apart from seeing comets as warning signs, many early astronomers thought that comets were balls of glowing gas high in Earth's atmosphere. However, once astronomers began comparing observation records internationally, they realized this idea was impossible. If comets were objects in our own planet's atmosphere, then in different parts of the world they would appear against different starry backdrops—different constellations would appear behind them. When astronomers compared notes, though, they found out this was not so. So, they finally concluded that comets were much farther away—*interplanetary* objects, traveling between the planets of our solar system.

Throughout the Middle Ages, though, no one made any real progress toward completing careful observations and basing interpretations strictly on observations. The growth of scientific approaches to science stalled during this period when superstition and pseudoscience were favored for most explanations. Then, in the fifteenth century, in Italy and Germany, several astronomers began to pioneer in making accurate measurements and records of the movements of comets.

The German astronomer Johann Müller (1436–1476), also known as Regiomontanus, began making systematic measurements of the movements of comets he observed, and in 1472, he recorded the movements of the comet that later became known as Halley's Comet. It was the first effort by a European scientist to bring the study of comets into the realm of science.

Girolamo Fracastoro (ca. 1478–1553), an Italian instructor in logic and anatomy, was the first to report the observation that the tail of a comet always points away from the Sun—even when the comet is moving away from the Sun. The German astronomer and mathematician Pierre Apian (1495–1552), also known as Petrus Apianus and Peter Bienewitz, made observations that agreed with Fracastoro—and wrote about them in a book he published in 1549. An illustration on the title page drew attention to the comet's tail always directed away from the Sun. This was an important scientific observation that reported objective facts and not suppositions, edging cometary observation out of the realm of superstition and astrology. In that book, Apian also described the appearances of five different comets. One of them turned out to be known later as Halley's Comet. A tiny scientific community and a legitimate scientific record were beginning to form.

In 1577 the great Danish astronomical observer Tycho Brahe (1546–1601) made arrangements for the observation of a bright comet from two separate locations at the same time. The two observatories were 375 miles (600 km) apart. Brahe used the observations to calculate the distance of the comet and concluded that it must be farther away than the Moon. That calculation was a clear blow against the idea that comets were fireballs tossed up into the atmosphere.

During the sixteenth century, Nicolaus Copernicus disproved the geocentric organization of the universe and published his book about it in 1543. It was many years before the new heliocentric theory was accepted, but Copernicus had made that first step. In 1609 German astronomer Johannes Kepler

The Danish astronomer Tycho Brahe, who made some of the first careful observations of comets, is depicted in his observatory, Uraniborg. To many Europeans of the Middle Ages, astronomers were akin to wizards.

(1571–1630) made some break-through observations about the nature of the orbits of the planets and set down the laws that govern them. In his book *New Astronomy,* published in Latin in 1609, Kepler proposed that, contrary to every precept he and others of his time had learned, the planets' orbits were not perfect circles. Instead, they were *ellipses.* That is, the planets traveled paths that looked something like squashed circles—decidedly imperfect looking. Instead of having one center, as a circle does, an ellipse has two foci (the plural of focus). The Sun, Kepler said,

The German astronomer Johannes Kepler (1571–1630) is remembered for discovering what are now referred to as Kepler's three laws of planetary motion. He saw a beautiful order in the way that the universe worked, referring to the movement of the heavenly bodies as the "music of the spheres."

was located at one of the two foci. Kepler stated this idea in what he called the first of his three laws of planetary motion.

Kepler's second law showed mathematically why the closer a planet is to the Sun, the faster it has to travel in its orbit. His third law stated that the square of any planet's period of revolution (the time it takes to travel) around the Sun is proportional to the cube of its distance from the Sun, meaning that the orbital period of a planet increases with the size of its orbit.

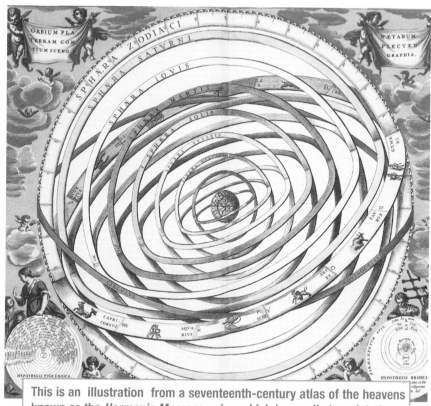

This is an illustration from a seventeenth-century atlas of the heavens known as the *Harmonia Macrocosmica*, which is usually translated as *The Harmony of the Universe*. The book was compiled by the cosmographer Andreas Cellarius. This illustration shows Tycho Brahe's view of the universe, in which the Moon and the Sun revolve around Earth and Mercury, Venus, Mars, Jupiter, and Saturn revolve around the Sun.

Kepler's three laws of planetary motion are important—but what Kepler did not try to do with them is equally important. Instead of trying to explain *why* something in nature took place, he simply tried to *describe* it in terms of mathematics. His method was a big departure from Greek and medieval approaches to nature and natural philosophy. Kepler dealt the final blow to the systems of Aristotle and Ptolemy, with their geocentric universe and perfectly circular orbits. Kepler had also set the groundwork for understanding how comets moved, but he didn't ever apply his laws to comets. That was for someone else to do.

Edmond Halley's Great Insight

In the following century, English physicist Isaac Newton (1642–1727) crafted his own set of laws, including watershed insights about gravity and how it works. He made use of his law of gravitation combined with Kepler's laws of planetary motion and came to the conclusion that the comet that appeared in 1680 (a "Sun-grazing" comet—one that orbits very close to the sun) was moving along a path that greatly resembled a parabola, curving around the Sun and then traveling along a curve that would never meet up again with the rest of the path. In other words, the comet would never return.

Meanwhile, Newton's good friend Edmond Halley (1656–1742), an English astronomer, became fascinated with comets and began gathering records. In 1705 he published a catalog of 24 comets and their orbits, based on Newton's and Kepler's calculations. The record showed the orbits to be in the form of parabolas. However, Halley saw that with more accurate measurements the orbits might prove to be very long ellipses instead. That is, Halley believed that comets might revolve around the Sun! He wrote that "the Space between the Sun and the fix'd Stars is so immense that there is Room enough for a Comet to revolve, tho' the Period of its Revolution be vastly long."

Remembered most for his explanation of gravity, Sir Isaac Newton (seen here) demonstrated that comets were objects acted upon by the same forces as the planets. Newton's friend, the astronomer Edmond Halley, applied Newton's work to correctly predict future appearances of the object now known as Halley's Comet.

Halley also noticed another important detail: Three of the comets in his catalog—the one that appeared in 1531 and reappeared in 1607 and 1682—seemed to travel almost exactly the same path. They also seemed to appear at a regular interval of 76 years. These "three comets," he concluded, were actually the same comet! He predicted his comet would appear again in 1758.

Halley unfortunately did not get to see how his prediction turned out. He died in 1742. However, several astronomers took up the project of searching for the comet. The French mathematician Alexis-Claude Clairaut (1713–1765) refined Halley's prediction to account for perturbations (disturbances) from Jupiter. He began his work in 1757 and raced against time to complete his refined prediction before the comet appeared. He had no computer, or even a calculator, for making the complicated calculations, so he talked several colleagues into helping him, including Joseph-Jérôme Lefrançais de Lalande. Lalande obtained the additional help of Madame Nicole-Reine Etable de la Brière Lépaute, the wife of King Louis XV's clock maker. The giant planet Jupiter influenced the comet's period

The answer to this question is not as obvious as it may seem. One answer might be "whatever it is that we study in science classes," or "whatever it is that scientists do to make a living." But these answers do not really say much.

Many people tend to think of science as a body of knowledge, a sort of file cabinet filled with facts that can be consulted when the need comes up. But how does one distinguish the facts from the fakes and fallacies?

It is the process of science that makes this profession unique—and remains the key to the usefulness of science. Even great scientists are not always right. They are pathfinders, trailblazers for those who come behind them. They succeed in raising new questions and point to new, surer ways of seeking answers, methods for finding the pieces of the giant jigsaw puzzle we call knowledge.

Science examines nature and attempts to explain some aspect of "how things work" in the natural universe. But the scientist's explanation is based on observation, examination, experiment, and the use of reason and logic in analyzing results. It must also be testable and other scientists must be able to obtain the same results by following the same steps.

Even then, a scientist's conclusions are tentative—not the final word. But they may be the piece that fits the puzzle best until a better piece of the puzzle turns up.

Last, science must be falsifiable. That is, it must be possible to show that the hypothesis is untrue if it is not true. For example, early astronomers had no way of examining a comet close-up. So, if they said comets were made of feathers or giant candles (not that anyone did), there would be no way of disproving what they said. For this reason, most early ideas about what comets were made of were not scientific because the statements were not falsifiable. However, early astronomers could examine and measure the movements of comets. From this information, they could draw conclusions about their positions—were they in Earth's atmosphere, or far out in the region of the planets? How often did they appear? Which way did the tail point as the comet rounded the Sun and began its return trip, traveling away from the Sun? These are some of the questions that could have falsifiable answers once Johann Müller and others began to collect observational facts and measurements.

So, when Johann Müller observed comets carefully, made systematic measurements of their movements, and recorded them, he was establishing a knowledge base that was based on observation and objective facts—not guesses or imaginative stories or unsubstantiated hearsay. And that is why science historians today say the work he did was science.

Halley's Comet streams across the sky, as viewed through the Uppsala Schmidt telescope.

in two ways—directly, by gravitational influence on the comet's path, and indirectly, by its influence on the Sun, which changed the Sun's position very slightly. Clairaut wanted to know the effect of Saturn, as well. The three mathematicians spent six months completing the calculations from sunup to sundown, every day. Finally, the work was finished, and Clairaut announced his prediction at the Academy of Sciences in Paris on November 14, 1758.

Meanwhile, a constant watch was kept by the master French astronomer Charles Messier (1730–1817), known as the "ferret of comets." He was working at the time as an assistant to another astronomer, Joseph-Nicolas Delisle. Messier found another comet in August, but he was plagued with skies too cloudy for observation in November and December of 1758. Finally, he spotted Halley's Comet on January 21, 1759. Strangely, for some reason that isn't clear, Delisle did not announce the discovery immediately.

However, as it turned out, a German amateur astronomer had already caught sight of the comet on December 25, 1758—weeks before Messier saw it. His name was Johann Georg Palitzsch, and he farmed in Prohlis, a village near Dresden, where the skies must have been clearer. So Palitzsch, not Messier, has the credit for finding the returning comet.

The comet had reappeared, as predicted, and it has been known as "Halley's Comet" ever since. Halley's Comet last appeared in 1986, and was first recorded in 239 B.C.E., as shown in Chinese accounts.

So began an enthusiasm for observations of Halley's Comet that has left an indelible mark on the science and study of comets. Once historians and astronomers knew how long the comet took to make its return trip (a span of time known as its period), they pored over old records looking for other mentions of it. They found many. However, according to comet astronomer John C. Brandt, the focus on Halley's Comet to the exclusion of others has its disadvantages. A great deal of data now exists on Halley's Comet, but in reality, says Brandt, "nature has taught us that every comet is an education," and no other comet is likely to be just like Halley. In fact, in the nineteenth century, many comets were observed, and from these observations, scientists began to see how different they could be. One comet, for example, has a period of only 3.3 years. Its name is Comet Encke, and it was first observed in 1786. It carries the name of the German astronomer Johann Franz Encke (1791–1865)—the first to give a prediction that it would return in 1822, which it did.

Comets come from distant areas of the solar system. Some come from as close as the outer solar system, others as far as the outer edge.

Where Do Comets Come From?

As Halley's work shows, in many ways, comets present a mathematical puzzle to scientists. They can see and plot part of a comet's orbit but not all. Then, in the case of a returning, or periodic, comet, scientists can time how long it takes to travel once around that orbit. They can clock how fast it was traveling in the solar system. Then they may need to make some adjustments for possible changes in speed. These and dozens of other mathematical considerations are part of the science of celestial mechanics. These kinds of calculations made possible Halley's prediction of his comet's return. Given all that—where did comets start out?

Only in the last century have scientists begun to agree on three main regions where comets originate—far out, farther out, and farthest out.

Far Out

The closest comets are those having orbits entirely within the outer solar system, between Uranus and Neptune, or even closer, in the region of Jupiter. Two comets known to lurk there are Chiron and Schwassmann-Wachmann 1. These are known as "short-period" comets because the period of time required for their return is under 200 years—much less in the case of these two.

Chiron is a nearly "dead" comet, that is, it no longer glows brightly as it approaches the Sun. Most of the gases have already blown out into space over the course of its travels. So, when astronomer Charles T. Kowal first discovered it in 1977, everyone thought Chiron was an asteroid. Its orbital period was measured in 1996 at 50.7 years. As a result, it received an asteroid number, 2060. However, if it was an asteroid, astronomers recognized, it was a strange one. Most asteroids orbit the Sun in a region known as the asteroid belt between Mars and Jupiter. No other asteroid known had an orbit so far from the Sun, between Saturn and Uranus.

Then astronomers began to notice that its light gray color was sometimes brighter and sometimes darker. For an asteroid, this was suspicious. In 1988 a group of astronomers who were observing asteroids noticed one night that Chiron was actually about twice as bright as usual. Over the following months,

Chiron continued to grow brighter—finally brightening to about three times its usual brightness. Other astronomers saw the same thing. They knew that Chiron was moving toward the Sun, and finally they realized that ice on Chiron was sublimating, changing into a gas that was catching the sunlight—just like a comet. Finally, astronomers concluded that Chiron is not an asteroid. It is a comet—just not a very active comet. Later, as months passed, the brightness grew dimmer.

Chiron is an odd asteroid, indeed. But it is also an odd comet. It is dark and it is very large, for a comet—up to 130 miles (200 km) in diameter. When astronomers looked back over old images of Chiron, they found evidence that the comet may have brightened suddenly in a similar outburst about 10 years earlier, in the late 1970s.

Another "far out" comet, Schwassmann-Wachmann 1, was discovered by two German skywatchers (Arnold Schwassmann and Arno Arthur Wachmann) in 1927. It has a period measured at 14.9 years in the late 1990s and its orbit is nearly circular and is very close in, for a comet—near Jupiter's orbit. It is very faint and difficult to see—unlike many comets that travel from much farther out—and it never gets closer to the sun than Jupiter. However, about once a year this comet erupts. Clouds and clouds of debris come spilling off its surface, and it brightens by about 300 times. When Schwassmann-Wachmann 1 does this, it can be seen with a telescope; just don't count on seeing it whenever you want—it is only really visible at unpredictable times. No one knows exactly what causes this "comet vomit." What makes it happen and what makes it happen on a cycle? It is an interesting topic for study.

Farther Out

Beyond the orbits of Neptune and Pluto lies a region filled with objects that went undetected for a long time. It is known as the Kuiper belt, named after the Dutch-born American astronomer Gerard P. Kuiper (1905–1973), who suggested its existence. (It is sometimes called the Edgeworth-Kuiper belt, also honoring the freelance astronomer Kenneth E. Edgeworth [1880–1972] from Ireland, who also suggested the idea.)

At first, the idea that there were objects orbiting the Sun in this region was just a theory. No one could see these dark, far-off bodies. They were too far away and had too little brightness to be detected by current instruments. Now, however, their existence is confirmed, thanks to the help of greatly improved instruments and new, very large telescopes. The objects in this region are often called KBOs (Kuiper belt objects) or trans-Neptunian objects (meaning, beyond Neptune's orbit).

Many astronomers think that short-period comets—such as Chiron and Schwassmann-Wachmann 1—formed originally in the Kuiper belt. At some point, the orbit becomes perturbed by Jupiter and the comet's movements begin to come closer to the Sun. So, Schwassmann-Wachmann 1 probably came from the Kuiper belt, and some astronomers think that Chiron originally came out of the Kuiper belt, as well.

Farthest Out

Long-period comets, such as Halley's Comet, return infrequently, usually taking more than 200 years for a round-trip. Others don't return at all. These comets must come from someplace even farther out at the edge of the solar system. The first to seriously investigate this problem was Jan Hendrick Oort (1900–1992). Oort was a Dutch astronomer famous for making major contributions to the understanding of our galaxy, its structure, and its rotation. Comets were almost a hobby for him, but he applied his considerable talent to the question as seriously as any other, and in 1950 he came up with a theory. Now widely accepted, Oort's theory suggested that a greatly distant cloud of "comet-stuff" lay at the edges of the solar system. Occasionally, he said, a piece of this comet material gets hurled inward, toward the Sun, possibly under the influence of passing stars. The distant cloud he envisioned at the border of interstellar space is now known as the "Oort Cloud."

According to calculations made by Oort, American astronomer Brian Marsden, and others, there may be as many as 100,000 million comets or more in that region. As few as 5 percent of those comets may be perturbed by passing stars. Some may get trapped in the solar system as short-period comets. Otherwise, they tend to get started on a long, eccentric orbit traveling in toward the Sun and then all the way back to the Oort Cloud. In any case, we see only a small fraction of the total number of comets that exist.

A question not answered by this theory is how the "comet-stuff" came to accrete (come together) and form bodies in this

How many people can spend their lives exploring the wonder of the universe? That is exactly what Dutch astronomer Jan Oort did. When Oort died in 1992, he was 92 years old, recognized worldwide as one of the twentieth century's greatest astronomers. Oort made landmark discoveries both by observing the universe—and by thinking about it, as a theorist.

When he was only in his twenties he showed that our galaxy—the Milky Way—rotates in a very special way. Each star in the galaxy moves independently of the others. Those close to the center rotate faster. Those at the edge rotate more slowly. The same is true of the planets in the solar system. Mercury, near the Sun and the center, travels very fast. Neptune, at the outer edge dawdles as it makes its journey around the Sun. Oort was also the first to recognize that the Sun is not at the center of our galaxy. In fact it's about halfway out toward the edge—at some 30,000 light years from the center, or nucleus.

Oort also discovered the existence of "dark matter," a mysterious substance that makes up about 90 percent of all matter yet gives off no light and reflects no light—so no one has ever seen it.

Even before radio astronomy came into use, Jan Oort recognized that radio waves could be used to find out facts about the universe. He had made calculations that led him to believe that star nurseries are nestled in the vast spiral arms of the galaxy, where huge clouds of hydrogen exist. Radio observatories confirmed that Oort was right about this, too.

For the study of comets, Oort's greatest contribution was the idea that a shell-like, spherical cloud surrounds the solar system. Within this cloud, he believed, roam perhaps as many as 100,000 million comets. Oort arrived at this idea by carefully studying the orbits of "long-period" comets—those that took a long time between visits to the inner solar system. According to his calculations, many of their orbits extended far beyond Pluto and the most distant portion of Neptune's orbit. This reservoir of comets became known as the "Oort Cloud," named in his honor.

Oort's interest—and his major contributions—extended over a remarkable variety and range of topics, from comets to stars and galaxies, and from our solar system to the large-scale structure of the universe. To him it was all exciting, and he wanted to see it all. As the last half of the twentieth century unfolded, he was in awe at how much more of the universe could be observed—with space telescopes such as the *Hubble Space Telescope* (*HST*) able to see almost to the beginning of time. (Even *HST*, though, cannot show the dark, small objects in the Oort Cloud.) Oort once wrote that he had spent his life marveling about the discoveries that lay ahead. A good title for his life story, he thought, would be *Looking Ahead in Wonder.*

This is a computer illustration of the formation of the Oort Cloud, which is believed to surround the solar system. The Oort Cloud is where the nuclei of comets are formed.

remote, immensely cold region, where matter was very sparse. So the Oort Cloud and the Kuiper belt pose exciting possibilities as reservoirs that supply the comets we see. However, scientists still are not really sure exactly where comets come from and how they happened to form.

A close-up view of a comet reveals the nucleus and rock and ice of the comet's core surface.

Chapter 4

Comet Close-up

The origins of comets—where they come from (or go to) and how they formed in the first place—have not been the only mystery. Not until the late twentieth century did scientists get a close-up look at a comet to see exactly what it was made of. What they saw was a surprise! By then, scientific observers had made considerable progress on understanding comets. However, many mysteries remained, and one of the most fundamental was the question of the composition of the comet nucleus—the only portion of a comet that remains throughout its lifetime.

Based on information gleaned from telescope observations and calculations, two models, or hypothetical structures, competed for attention. One, called the "sandbank" model, suggested that the comet nucleus is made up of a loose swarm of ice and dust. According to the sandbank model, as the comet approaches the Sun, the heating of this swarm produces the comet tail and coma. The other model, proposed by British astronomer Fred Whipple, envisioned a solid body at the heart of the coma, a nucleus of water ice impregnated with rock and dust. He called it the "dirty snowball" model.

Many astronomers leaned toward Whipple's model. For one thing, Sun-grazing comets came very close to the heat of the Sun and then traveled on to return another day. How could they survive the close encounter with the Sun's great heat without disintegrating if there were no solid body at the center? Secondly, radar echoes bounced off Comet Encke seemed to indicate the presence of a solid body. Finally, the date when a comet actually passes closest to the Sun remains elusive to calculations—often advancing or slowing by a day or two. This phenomenon seemed best explained by jets of dust and gas streaming irregularly from cracks in a solid body—and slowing or hastening arrival in the vicinity of the Sun.

ICE: The First Mission to a Comet

Once a spacecraft is launched, sometimes investigators and engineers team up to find extra duties it can perform, once its job is done. That is exactly what happened to *ISEE-3* (*International Sun/Earth Explorer 3*), one of three solar observers launched in 1978. By 1982, its job of observing the solar wind and the relationship between Sun and Earth at the

For centuries after the invention of the telescope, the optical lenses of big telescopes were among the astronomer's best tools for watching comets. (The watchful eyes of amateur astronomers have always also been a great boon to comet astronomy—and they still are today.) In addition, in the last 50 years astronomers have gained a few new, exciting tricks for watching comets.

The first telescopes gathered light and allowed us to see objects that were too distant and too dim to see with the naked eye. However, Isaac Newton showed that sunlight breaks down into a spectrum of colors. Later, scientists discovered that sunlight is only the visible part of a much larger spectrum of radiation types that the human eye cannot see. These invisible types of radiation range from very short-frequency gamma rays and ultraviolet radiation on one end of the spectrum to infrared radiation on the other end. Visible light is about in the middle. So, among the most useful instruments for seeing the universe and its objects are spectrometers—used to "see" other kinds of radiation.

During the nineteenth and early twentieth century, scientists became expert at decomposing sunlight into its constituents. They soon discovered that, in addition to the spectrum of colors, a more exacting spectrometer showed that sunlight emissions also produced dark lines in the spectra (plural of spectrum). By comparing these spectrographs with experiments with elements found on Earth, they discovered that each chemical element produces a different set of dark lines, called absorption lines. And this produced a powerful key to understanding the composition of the far-distant objects of the solar system, the galaxy, and the universe. Today, spacecraft exploring the solar system commonly carry at least two types of spectrometers, an ultraviolet spectrometer and an infrared spectrometer.

Infrared Spectrometer: Infrared spectrometry allows us to view objects in the universe that are so cool they are dim and do not give off much visible light. In the case of examining a comet, infrared imaging spectroscopy can help map the composition of the nucleus of a comet with sufficient detail to see craters and other large geologic features and to determine their composition.

An infrared spectrometer can also act as a very sophisticated thermometer. It can determine the distribution of heat energy a body is emitting, allowing scientists to determine the temperature of that body or substance.

Ultraviolet (UV) Spectrometer: "Near" UV radiation—the longest UV wavelengths—can pass through the Earth's atmosphere and give you a sunburn. But atoms and molecules absorb shorter-wavelength "far" UV radiation more easily than any other kind of radiation, so UV radiation is for the most part blocked by Earth's atmosphere. As a result, UV spectrometers cannot function very well for viewing astronomical objects from the ground. However, on a spacecraft, the UV spectrometer functions as a very specialized type of light meter that is sensitive to ultraviolet light. Because atoms and molecules absorb UV radiation so well, spaceborne UV telescopes equipped with spectrometers are the best way to observe atoms in the universe—to see what chemical elements stars and other objects are made of and to detect diffuse interstellar and intergalactic gas. The UV spectrometer enables scientists to identify the presence of particular atoms or ions and deduce what physical processes are going on.

Charge-Coupled Devices (CCDs): A CCD uses a light-sensitive substance mounted on a silicon chip to record images digitally, taking the place of a camera. The imaging instruments carried by most cometary spacecraft are capable of sending back clear images of a comet's nucleus, as the spacecraft speeds through the comet's dusty, gaseous head. CCDs are able to show details the size of an automobile, such as rocks only 4 yards (3.6 m) across. They are able to record objects so faint that a conventional telescope would have to have an aperture 10 times as large to detect them. CCD images can also be uploaded to computers for analysis and automated searches.

Comet Hyakutake was visible from many parts of the world in 1996. The comet was named after its discoverer, Yuji Hyakutake, who discovered it using a pair of binoculars. "I don't care about the naming of the comet," Hyakutake said. "If many people could enjoy that comet, that is the happiest thing for me."

Hubble Space Telescope. The *Hubble Space Telescope* is a satellite telescope that orbits Earth. Astronomers can train its cameras and instruments on far-distant objects with exciting results. However, *Hubble* has also had excellent success observing objects closer at home—right here in our solar system. Hubble took images of Comet Hyakutake on March 25, 1996, when the comet passed close to Earth, within 9.5 million miles (15 million km). The results were unusually clear images of the region of the coma close to the nucleus.

ROSAT Satellite. The ROSAT satellite (named ROSAT after Wilhelm Conrad Roentgen [1845–1923], the discoverer of X rays: ROentgen SATellite) was designed to measure X-ray emissions as it orbited Earth from 1990 to 1999. While exploring other objects in the universe, scientists thought it would be interesting to catch some images of the Comet Hyakutake as it was passing through in March 1996. Did comets emit X rays? No one knew for sure, but scientists thought they might—so they took a look. Among the images taken by ROSAT, for the first time ever scientists saw an image showing X-ray emissions from a comet. The ROSAT satellite image showed X-ray emissions from Comet Hyakutake that were 100 times the intensity expected by scientists. There were also strong increases and decreases—another surprise!

What caused these unexpected X rays? The X rays shifted from stronger to weaker and back to stronger, but they always came from the same area—a crescent-shaped region in front of the moving comet. In 1997 a group of scientists analyzed the data using computer programs—a process they call computer modeling—and they came to the conclusion that the X rays were probably caused by an interaction between the solar wind (ions streaming away from the Sun) and atoms and molecules surrounding the comet.

boundaries of Earth's *magnetosphere* (the region around Earth where Earth's magnetic field affects the flow of ions from the solar wind) was finished. So NASA engineers retooled its trajectory, or path, and headed it off for a whole new life. Now dubbed *ICE* (*International Cometary Explorer*), this spacecraft became the first mission ever sent to observe a comet—and in fact, it observed not one, but two comets. On June 5, 1985,

ICE swung behind Comet Giacobini-Zinner at a distance of about 16,500 miles (26,550 km) and collected particles from the comet's plasma tail that *ICE* analyzed using its instruments. Then on September 11, 1985, *ICE* collected its first data about the comet itself. It was the first time any mission had had the opportunity to study a comet and its surroundings *in situ* (on the spot). The spacecraft found a region where charged particles from the comet were interacting with particles from the solar wind. It also detected a tail about 15,500 miles (25,000 km) wide composed of *plasma* (a gaslike substance with both positive and negative particles in almost complete balance). *ICE* detected evidence of the presence of water molecules and carbon monoxide ions—and that was the first direct confirmation of the "dirty snowball" theory about the nature of the nucleus. The spacecraft flew within 4,880 miles (7,862 km) of the comet and, even though NASA engineers were worried, it suffered very little damage from the dust surrounding the nucleus. (This could have been a big problem, since *ICE* was never planned for such a mission and had no dust protection at all.)

The following year, *ICE* joined five other spacecraft from several nations in an internationally coordinated observation of Comet Halley. *ICE* made its observations on March 28, 1986, but could get no closer than 19 million miles (31 million km). Still, the spacecraft was able to collect data about the solar wind "upstream" from the comet (on the Sun-side). The most distant flyby of all the missions to Halley, *ICE* still made history with its flyby of Comet Giacobini-Zinner and then went on to do a job no one had imagined when the spacecraft was launched.

In 2014, *ICE* may return to Earth's vicinity and NASA may try to bring the stalwart spacecraft back home. If that works, NASA has already promised the spacecraft to the Smithsonian Institution for exhibit.

The Soviet Union's Vega Missions

The Soviet Union (now Russia and several nearby countries) also restructured a pair of space missions already planned to visit Venus and sent them both on to visit Comet Halley, as well. The spacecraft were designed much like the previous Soviet missions to Venus, *Venera 9* and *Venera 10*. *Vega 1* was launched December 15, 1984, with *Vega 2* following six days later, on December 21. They both arrived at Venus in June the following year. Each of these spacecraft had three parts: a flyby spacecraft to collect atmospheric data; a balloon probe to study the composition, temperature, and movement of the atmosphere; and a lander to study the planet's surface. The two balloons and two landers were released and descended into the thick atmosphere of Venus, where they transmitted data until they were finally destroyed by the crushing atmospheric pressure.

After collecting data from the balloons, the two flyby spacecraft continued on to rendezvous with Comet Halley. *Vega 1* arrived first, beginning to take images as early as March 4, 1986, and making its closest approach on March 6, 1986. These images were used by the planners for *Giotto*, the

The Soviet Union's *Vega 2* probe obtained this image of the nucleus of Halley's Comet. It was one of the first clear images of a comet's nucleus ever obtained.

European Space Agency's spacecraft, for planning its closest approach within a few days.

The first images from *Vega 1* showed two bright spots, and at first scientists thought that Comet Halley had a double nucleus. Later, though, the two bright spots turned out to be two jets of gas that were spewing dust and gases from the interior of the nucleus. The nucleus also looked dark in the images and the infrared spectrometer showed a nuclear temperature of 80–260°F (300–400 K)—surprisingly high for a small, icy body.

Vega 2 arrived three days after *Vega 1*, on March 9. *Vega 2* flew a little closer to the comet nucleus—coming within 4,990 miles (8,030 km). *Vega 2* also began imaging immediately and collected slightly sharper pictures because it was closer.

Giotto: Just for Halley

In 1301 the Italian painter Giotto di Bondone looked up at the skies and used as a model the comet we now know was Comet Halley. (It would be centuries before Halley would do his research linking this and the other comets that turned out to be the same.) The artist was painting the Star of Bethlehem in his painting *Adoration of the Magi*, completed in 1304. So, nearly 700 years later the European Space Agency (ESA), an international cooperative program, gave Giotto's name to its mission to Comet Halley.

The Giotto mission was planned specifically for visiting comets—and after Halley in 1986, *Giotto* would extend its mission to visit another one, Comet Grigg-Skjellerup, in

Since ancient times, humankind has regarded comets as supernatural signs of extraordinary events. In the *Adoration of the Magi*, the early Italian Renaissance painter Giotto depicted as a comet the star that led the wise men to the manger where the Christ Child was born.

1992. For the Halley mission, *Giotto* took the first close-up images of a comet's nucleus. It determined what elements and isotopes comprised the gases and dust of the coma. It explored the chemical and physical processes, going on to examine the comet's atmosphere and ionosphere. It made measurements of the dust and gases of the nucleus. And it investigated the relationship between the plasma surrounding the comet and the solar wind.

Giotto was designed to go in closer to the comet nucleus than any of the other missions, and it came within 370 miles (600 km). At first, everything seemed to be going fine. The spacecraft began sending images to Earth. They showed that Halley was shaped like a peanut and had two jets spewing bright material. The dust impacts seemed minimal, then suddenly, wham! The best guess is that the spacecraft crossed through one of the jets and got peppered by dust particles that

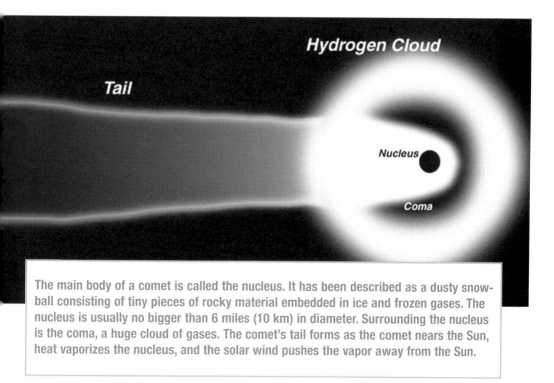

The main body of a comet is called the nucleus. It has been described as a dusty snowball consisting of tiny pieces of rocky material embedded in ice and frozen gases. The nucleus is usually no bigger than 6 miles (10 km) in diameter. Surrounding the nucleus is the coma, a huge cloud of gases. The comet's tail forms as the comet nears the Sun, heat vaporizes the nucleus, and the solar wind pushes the vapor away from the Sun.

swung it out of position for communicating with Earth. Engineers worked for 30 minutes before they could get it lined up again. Some damage had been done, but *Giotto* had done a great job of collecting information just the same.

Giotto's information showed that the material Halley was throwing out into surrounding space was mostly water—about 80 percent by volume. The spacecraft found seven jets that among them were spewing some 3 tons of material per second. *Giotto* also provided data that showed that the surface of the comet was covered with a layer of organic material (molecules combining carbon and hydrogen, some of the raw materials of life).

Twins from Japan

Japan also launched twin spacecraft. Those missions were designed to measure the effects of Comet Halley on the space environment as it made its way toward the Sun. The second, *Suisei* (meaning "comet" in Japanese), launched on August 18, 1985, and began its observations of Halley first, in November 1985, before its twin reached the area. *Suisei* made observations of ultraviolet emissions from the comet—as many as six images each day up to its closest approach on March 8, 1986. Then *Suisei*'s UV instrument was turned off and the solar wind experiment began measuring the comet's interactions with the solar wind. *Suisei*, like *ICE*, also detected water and carbon monoxide, plus carbon dioxide ions. The spacecraft took a few hits, but succeeded in detecting several outbursts of jets from the comet as it turned on its axis.

The first of the twins, *Sakigake* (meaning "pioneer" in Japanese), lifted off January 7, 1985. To add to the knowledge base about comets, its goal was to measure ions in the solar wind, plasma wave spectra, and the magnetic field in the vicinity of Comet Halley as it flew by. It came closest on March 11, 1986, but only at a distance of 4.5 million miles (7 million km). *Sakigake* also helped act as a reference for *Giotto* as the ESA spacecraft prepared for its close approach.

Composite View

The Halley observations—coordinated by many countries and making use of several spacecraft—provided an exciting look at the famous Comet Halley. Edmond Halley had always encouraged international cooperation among scientists and pooling of resources. So, it was fitting that his comet was the object of this unprecedented international space effort. Never before had so many countries cooperated in any space observation. This coordinated examination by multiple spacecraft provided a set of close-up visible-light images, UV spectra, on-the-spot measurements of the comet's tail and coma and their interactions with the solar wind, and more. *Giotto* discovered a magnetic cavity surrounding Halley's Comet, a detail never detected before—or since. That is, the magnetic field in that area was practically zero, a real surprise. Also, for the first time scientists saw what a comet nucleus looks like up close. Its irregular peanut shape made sense because the comet is too small to keep material from blowing off its surface. Scientists could also see that the nucleus had craters and other surface features. Always before, these traits had been hidden behind the bright veils of the coma and tail. They found out that evaporation occurred only from specific jets, or vents, in the surface. The comparatively huge size of the coma was startling—100,000 miles (161,000 km) across—compared with the tiny nucleus, the heart of the comet, which measured only 15 miles (24 km) in diameter. They also verified that the gases of the coma include ionized hydrogen, carbon, nitrogen, water, and carbon monoxide, among others. From these measurements scientists can see more accurately what the nucleus is made of, and also obtain confirmation of measurements of the coma's spectra previously gained from instruments on Earth.

Another surprise was the dark color of the nucleus, not the image of the icy snowball they had anticipated. This dirty snowball is inky black, as if the ice were covered with carbon. Many of the dark particles found were similar to compounds found in carbonaceous chondrites, a type of primitive meteorite sometimes found on Earth. The comet was also rich in particles containing carbon, hydrogen, oxygen, and nitrogen—all essential, at least on Earth, to the existence of life. Some scientists think that comets may be the source of these meteorites and may even have brought the building blocks of life to Earth's surface long ago.

Comets Up Close

At the dawn of the twenty-first century, several new missions began the planning stages. One has already completed its mission. This time the visitor was a little experimental spacecraft called *Deep Space 1*, launched in October 1998. This small traveler's main purpose was to test a new propulsion system, but after that job was done, it made a risky detour to visit a comet named Borrelly. On the way, *Deep Space 1* had to dodge thick clouds of comet dust that could have ended its voyage. Then, traveling inside the comet's coma, it made its closest approach on September 22, 2001.

The images *Deep Space 1* sent back were the best yet, and the rest of its scientific data were also exciting. The spacecraft took black-and-white pictures, infrared measurements, data on ions and electrons, and measurements of the magnetic field and plasma waves around the comet. It explored the size of the comet, the nature of its surface, its brightness, its mass, and its density. It measured and identified the gases surrounding the comet, and measured the interaction of the solar wind with the comet.

(To find out about the other upcoming missions as of June 2003 turn to the last chapter of this book.)

This is an illustration of the astronomical event of Comet Shoemaker-Levy 9 colliding with Jupiter.

Chapter 5

Colliding Words

W hat happens when a comet hits a planet? Scientists got front-row seats to just such a collision in 1994, when a comet called Shoemaker-Levy 9 (SL-9) broke up into pieces and smashed smack into the great gaseous planet of Jupiter. It was, as one astronomer put it, "The astronomical event of the century." It was also, without question, the best-documented solar system collision ever.

Front Seat at a Smashing Event

In May 1993 astronomers realized that an extraordinary event was about to take place. A comet named Shoemaker-Levy 9 was on a collision course for the giant planet Jupiter. The comet was going to smash directly into this enormous gas

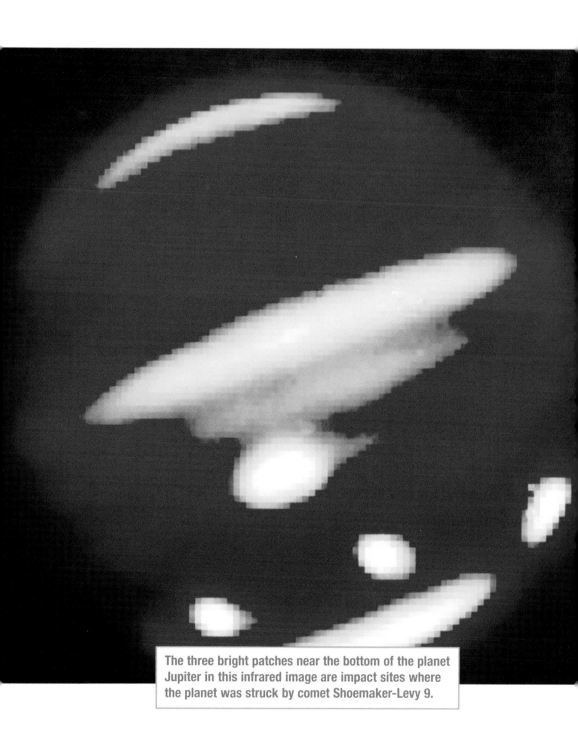

The three bright patches near the bottom of the planet Jupiter in this infrared image are impact sites where the planet was struck by comet Shoemaker-Levy 9.

giant. No one had ever observed anything like this before. It was a chance in a lifetime to see what would happen.

Why was this event so rare? Most comets have very large, elliptical orbits that loop far out to the edge of the solar system and zoom in to curve around the Sun. While some do have shorter orbits, Shoemaker-Levy 9's orbit was unusual. Comet Shoemaker-Levy 9 had somehow become caught in Jupiter's gravitational field. Scientists began piecing together what had happened. Apparently, Comet Shoemaker-Levy 9 had already passed close to Jupiter several times. Each time, the giant planet had robbed some of the comet's momentum. Eventually, the comet was pulled out of its long, elliptical orbit around the Sun. It began to orbit Jupiter, instead.

As scientists continued to study Comet Shoemaker-Levy 9, they learned that on July 7, 1992, the comet came so close to Jupiter that it had been pulled apart into many fragments. By tugging at the fragile ball, Jupiter's immense gravitational field had produced tensions (known as "tidal stress") in the ball of ice and rock. Finally the fragile comet became so wracked by the huge planet's influence that it flew apart.

Torn to Pieces

In recent years, scientists have realized that few comets or asteroids are cohesive, tightly packed objects. Usually, they have been smacked around over and over as they sail through the solar system—often disintegrating and reassembling. Some may never have fused into a single body in the first place. So they are roving "rubble piles," as Eugene and

Carolyn Shoemaker, two of the three codiscoverers of SL-9, once put it.

By the time Comet Shoemaker-Levy 9 was identified on photographic plates, it was bar-shaped and had several tails. Two wings of dust extended from each end of the bar. Within a few weeks, an extremely powerful ground-based telescope had captured an image of the comet. The image showed that the "bar" actually consisted of a series of nuclei that looked like a string of pearls.

Comet Shoemaker-Levy 9 had been torn apart into pieces—21 pieces at best count. Tidal stress had torn it apart. When it became obvious that this string of ice chunks was headed straight for Jupiter, scientists began to marshal their resources to record the spectacular event from every possible angle. They calculated the impact date and made sure they could use *HST* to look. It was such an important once-in-a-lifetime event that they had no problem getting permission.

Countdown to Impact

That's where the Hubble Space Telescope came in. On July 12, 1994, the comet was known to be nearing Jupiter's large magnetosphere, an area filled with electromagnetic radiation and electrically charged particles. On this date, the *Hubble Space Telescope* observed dramatic changes in the magnetosphere. For about 2 minutes, *Hubble* detected a large quantity of magnesium—one of the major elements present in comet dust. About 18 minutes later, a significant change took place in the light reflected from the dust particles in Comet Shoemaker-Levy

9. From these signals scientists knew that at least one of the comet fragments had entered the cloud tops of Jupiter.

Some scientists expected the comet fragments to be torn apart into even smaller pieces shortly before impact. They thought the giant planet's huge tidal forces would stretch the pieces until they disintegrated.

Hubble's observations came into play again, just 10 hours before impact. This time *HST* took a stunning image of the comet's fragments stretched out in a long row, each one distinct and solid. To most planetary scientists this was a strong piece of evidence that the pieces did not disintegrate. The freight train of fragments hit, one "car" at a time— moving at a speed of about 40 miles (60 km) per second. The first pieces hit on July 16, 1994, followed by four more on July 17. A few more fragments crashed into the giant planet's atmosphere each day for 6 days.

As each fragment hit Jupiter's atmosphere, it threw up a titanic fireball. Some of the fireballs had temperatures as high as about 32,000°F (18,000°C). Brightness in the area increased by as much as 15 percent as each piece struck the planet

Scientists think that the fireballs represented only a small fraction of the total energy output from the blasts. Most of that energy was probably absorbed by Jupiter's atmosphere. When comet fragments containing high proportions of ice hit the planet, they sent plumes of water spewing into space.

Within 30 minutes, huge black clouds began to form where the fireballs had been. These dark spots looked like pancakes in Jupiter's atmosphere. Some measured up to 6,000 miles

(10,000 km) across. More than one cloud was large enough to swallow up the entire Earth. The blemishes were still visible months after the collision, although the planet's constant easterly and westerly winds soon curled their edges. Eventually, the scars faded from Jupiter's complexion.

The *Hubble Space Telescope*'s study of the mysterious dark clouds revealed a high content of sulfur-bearing compounds. Most of these compounds seemed to disperse within a few days. The ammonia in the spots took several months to dissipate. The dark areas also contained silicon, magnesium, and iron—substances not found in Jupiter's atmosphere. They must have come from the comet fragments.

The impact of one fragment known as "K" created spectacular aurorae in a different location from Jupiter's usual light shows. (Aurorae are magnificent luminous displays of color that are caused on Earth by interaction between Earth's atmosphere and the solar wind. On Jupiter, though, the atmospheric atoms give beautiful colored arcs and structures when excited by energetic charged particles trapped in Jupiter's magnetosphere.) Planetary scientists believe that when K hit Jupiter's atmosphere, it created an electromagnetic disturbance in the planet's magnetosphere.

Observing a Smash Hit

Comet Shoemaker-Levy 9 smashed into the nightside of Jupiter—the side turned away from Earth at the time. So Earth-based astronomers had no hope of seeing the event directly. However, in addition to using *HST*, both professional and amateur astronomers found ways to observe its effects.

Scientists watched the edge of Jupiter's disk for signs of the impact. They observed the dark spots in the cloud tops as the planet rotated and the area that had been struck came into view. They also used instruments to measure changes in Jupiter's magnetosphere.

Three spacecraft, *Voyager 2*, *Galileo*, and *Ulysses*, also helped scientists study the collision. *Voyager 2* had finished its missions to Jupiter, Saturn, Uranus, and Neptune long before and was on its way out of the solar system. It was nearly 4 billion miles (6 billion km) away. Nevertheless, the spacecraft used its ultraviolet spectrometer and planetary radio astronomy instrument to detect, time, and measure impact-related emissions from Jupiter.

Galileo was the only spacecraft with a direct view of the nightside areas where the comet pieces hit. Even though it was about 150 million miles (240 million km) from Jupiter, *Galileo* was close enough. It recorded the events as well as the best Earth-based telescopes would have done—if the collision had been visible from Earth.

At the time of the collision, *Ulysses* was making a swing past the southern pole of the Sun, but it could see Jupiter fine from there, and it gathered useful information. Scientists used the spacecraft's combined radio and plasma wave instrument to search for radio emissions caused by the Comet Shoemaker-Levy 9 impacts.

The series of collisions was tremendously exciting, but it was also sobering. The impacts released more energy into Jupiter's atmosphere than the energy of all Earth's nuclear arsenals combined. They had an enormous effect on the giant planet's atmosphere, and the clear message for Earth was: If it can happen on Jupiter, it can also happen here.

Target: Earth

Shoemaker-Levy 9 is not the first object ever to hit Jupiter, nor will it be the last. Also, Jupiter is certainly not the only object in the solar system that a comet or asteroid has ever hit. Have you ever taken a good look at the Moon? All those craters represent hits made by objects large and small as they smashed into the Moon's surface. Every object in the solar system has received thousands of hits since the solar system first formed. In fact, over the 4.5 billion years since Earth first formed, many objects have also hit our own planet.

Tunguska, Russia

Most of the big hits happened a long time ago, eons before humans lived on Earth. However, occasionally a small "space rock"—a piece of a comet or an asteroid—makes its way through the resistance of Earth's atmosphere and hits. Most of the time, this happens in the ocean or in an unpopulated area, and the rock is small.

On the morning of June 30, 1908, though, a huge and startling explosion took place in the forests of Siberia, near a village called Tunguska. Sounds like thunder were heard far

On June 30, 1908, the explosion of a fireball in the sky over the Tunguska River valley in Siberia leveled more than 2,000 square miles of forest. Scientists now believe that the explosion was a meteoroid breaking up in the atmosphere.

away, across the expanses of the Siberian tundra, to the east, in St. Petersburg, Russia. In Oslo, Norway, in the skies still dark with night, a strange light shone on the eastern horizon. In England, a woman later recorded that she saw a pale, rosy glow in the sky at midnight, when the skies should have been pitch black. A reddish glow remained in the skies the following night throughout most of Europe.

At the time, Russia was on the brink of revolution, and the area near Tunguska was remote. No one went to investigate for several years—not until 1924. Scientists talked to witnesses— a few reindeer herders had been camped nearby. Most of them were deaf for the rest of their lives, and one man died from the force of the blast. Still no one actually went to the site until 1927, nearly 20 years after the blast. What the investigators saw was chilling.

Apparently the object fell through the skies and exploded just before it would have hit the ground. Trees in a roughly circular region about 36 miles (58 km) across were felled like toothpicks thrown out from the center of the blast. At the center, the trees still stood, but their branches were stripped.

For years, scientist were unsure whether the blast was caused by an incoming comet or an asteroid. Current opinion favors the asteroid theory because of fragments found in the trees by investigators. However, a small comet would have done the same kind of damage. The object was probably a stony asteroid, about 150 to 200 feet (50 to 60 m) across— about half the size of a football field. If the object had fallen in a populated area, it would have done tremendous damage, and many lives would have been lost.

The Death of the Dinosaurs

Another hit, much earlier in Earth's history, was even larger and much more devastating. It happened long before any human beings existed on Earth, at a time when dinosaurs ruled the lands. They roamed Earth's surface for 160 million

Craters on Earth

Vital Statistics

Location	Approximate Age in Years	Approximate Diameter of Crater
BARRINGER CRATER (METEOR CRATER) WINSLOW, ARIZONA	50,000	3,960 feet (1,200 m)
ODESSA, TEXAS	50,000	528 feet (161 m)
CHICXULUB, MEXICO	65 million	62 miles (100 km)
MJØLNIR CRATER, SCANDINAVIA	150 million	1.25 miles (2 km)
BARENTS SEA MANICOUAGAN, QUEBEC, CANADA	212 million	62 miles (100 km)
LAKE ACRAMAN, AUSTRALIA	570 million	100 miles (160 km)
BEAVERHEAD, MONTANA	600 million	40 miles (60 km)
SUDBURY, ONTARIO, CANADA	1.85 billion	125 miles (200 km)
VREDEFORT, SOUTH AFRICA	1.97 billion	90 miles (140 km)

years. (Human beings have been around for a much shorter time—only 200,000 years, a tiny blip in the history of our planet.) Then the dinosaurs disappeared. Paleontologists had found their bones and had reconstructed some of their history, but no one was sure why they had disappeared.

The Chicxulub event is the term scientists use to refer to the collision of an asteroid with the Yucatán Peninsula some 65 million years ago. Scientists believe the event led to the extinction of the dinosaurs.

Geologists could tell from the fossil record in Earth's layered crust that the end had come suddenly. The record showed 160 million years of dinosaur bones and then, suddenly, nothing more.

In the last 20 years scientists have found very strong evidence that an asteroid or comet about 6 miles (10 km) wide hit Earth's surface about where the Yucatán Peninsula curves around the Gulf of Mexico today, near where a small village called Chicxulub now stands. The event happened 65 million years ago—the same time that the dinosaurs disappeared from the fossil record. A hit that large, scientists estimate, would have created a raging, roaring fireball as the object thundered through the atmosphere. Then, with a giant explosion, it would have plunged into the planet's crust, and the waters of the oceans would have swelled into violent tidal waves. The air, searing with heat, would have caused forest fires all around the site, and huge plumes of smoke, dust, and debris would have flown upward into the atmosphere, to be transported around the world. The dark clouds of smoke and dust would have caused the skies to darken and block out the Sun. Animals that did not die outright, would die from starvation when plants could not grow. The food chain would disintegrate. Scientists estimate that 90 percent of all organisms living on Earth at that time became extinct within about 100 years.

The Watch

Comet and asteroid hits like the ones just described do not happen often—in the case of the Chicxulub event, not more often than once in 50 million to 100 million years. However, scientists have recognized that an early warning system would help humankind survive small- to medium-sized hits. So, around the world, scientists have begun to keep a constant vigil as they watch for "Near Earth Objects," or NEOs, that might now be or might one day move into a collision course with Earth. Several teams of scientists have set up constant surveillance and spend most of their professional time on the NEO watch. Their efforts center primarily on asteroids, some of which cross Earth's orbit as they travel around the Sun. Many of them are so dark and small that they have not yet been spotted or cataloged or had their orbits calculated. However, comets also pose a threat. Comet Hale-Bopp, when it was first discovered in 1995, gave watchers a start. Hale-Bopp was beyond the orbit of Jupiter at the time of its discovery, some 7.15 AU. (AU stands for "astronomical unit—the distance from Earth to the Sun, or 93 million miles [150 million km].) Ordinarily, most amateur telescopes would not show a comet as far away as that. Hale-Bopp was big. It was at least 25 miles (40 km) in diameter. That is, it was four times bigger than the asteroid that caused the death of the dinosaurs.

The NASA spacecraft *ICE* was the first to ever observe a comet up-close. NASA hopes to feature it one day in the Smithsonian Institution in Washington, DC.

Finding Out
More . . .

The ancient occupation of comet watching continues, alive and well today. Amateurs and professional astronomers alike scan the skies for signs of a new comet that no one has ever seen before. It is an exciting vigil. As a comet travels its long route from the edge of the solar system, it suddenly arrives within view. Day by day, the speck of light grows brighter. It forms its "hairy tail." Then once it has paid its visit to Earth's part of the solar system and the Sun, the visitor leaves.

However, now that human beings have a way to visit comets and see them close-up, "paying a visit" works both ways. Knowledge about comets has grown enormously since spacecraft have begun paying visits to comets. Both NASA in the United States and other organizations, including ESA, have future visits planned. So, future knowledge is sure to grow by even greater leaps and bounds.

Stardust to Wild-2

On February 7, 1999, NASA's *Stardust* spacecraft began its long journey with a launch by rocket from Cape Canaveral in Florida. It is headed for a comet called Wild-2—called that because it is the second comet discovered by astronomer Paul Wild (pronounced Vilt).

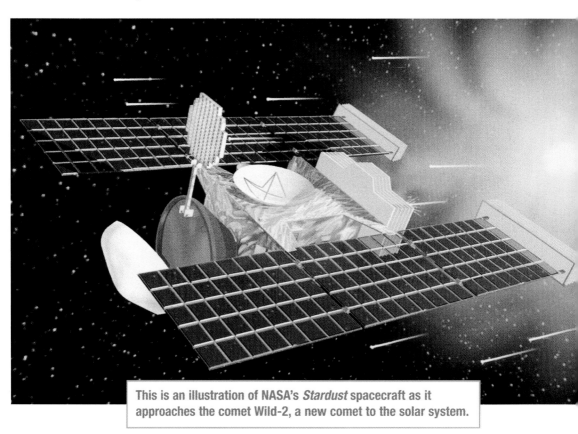

This is an illustration of NASA's *Stardust* spacecraft as it approaches the comet Wild-2, a new comet to the solar system.

Wild-2 started out in the outer solar system—traveling an orbit between Jupiter and Uranus. However, in 1974, it came fairly close to Jupiter in its travels. It was 10 times farther away than Shoemaker-Levy 9 was in 1994 when that comet was torn apart and plunged into Jupiter's clouds. However, Wild-2 came within 0.006 AU of Jupiter—close enough to the influence of the giant planet that it ended up traveling a different orbit. Now Wild-2's orbit skims inside the orbit of Mars during its closest approach to the Sun. Paul Wild spotted the small, dim comet on its next tour close enough to Earth to be seen. It came within 1.21 AU of Earth on January 6, 1978. The best view since then was March 1997, when it came within 0.85 AU of Earth. It was brighter than in the past as well (because it was closer to the Sun) and could be seen with most backyard telescopes.

Why visit such a small, unexciting comet? Wild-2 had been cooling in the icebox of the outer solar system for about 4.56 billion years, up until it got bounced closer to the Sun by Jupiter in 1974. The comet then swung into its new orbit, making its first appearance in 1978. So Wild-2 is a relatively new comet to the inner solar system. Because it has only orbited close to the Sun a few times, not very much of its volatile dust and gases has boiled away yet. When *Stardust* encounters Wild-2 in 2004, the comet will have made only five close passes by the Sun. That's not very many times, compared with, say, Halley's Comet, which has journeyed past the Sun more than 100 times based on observations and estimates.

There's another interesting reason for visiting Wild-2. *Stardust's* flight path could be planned to intersect Wild-2's orbit at the right moment so that *Stardust* can fly by very slowly—at only about 13,600 miles (21,900 km) per hour. This will give the spacecraft a chance to scoop up some comet dust from Wild-2's coma and bring it home. *Stardust* will not fly very close to Wild-2, just about 95 mi (150 km) away. That way, it won't be overwhelmed by too much dust, but should encounter enough to scoop some up. A visit to most comets would require a higher velocity flyby and the comet dust would just blow out the back end of the spacecraft. So, Wild-2 will be in just the right place at just the right time.

Since comets are thought to be primitive leftover material from the early solar system, this opportunity to retrieve a sample of comet dust is especially exciting. From these samples, scientists hope to find out more about the formation of the universe. Because they are unchanged and unweathered, their nuclei are believed to consist of the oldest material scientists have ever had the chance to examine.

Stardust should also get good pictures of the nucleus—its resolution will be about three times greater than the resolution achieved by *Giotto* during the flyby at Halley's Comet in 1986.

In 2006 *Stardust* will return to Earth, sending its sample collectors down by parachute. It will be the first sample return ever from a comet, and scientists will be able to examine the composition of the samples in detail—almost as good a deal as going there themselves!

The *Rosetta* Mission

The *Rosetta* Mission is an ambitious mission to the Comet Wirtanen, planned by the European Space Agency (ESA). It was due to launch in January 2003, and was expected to arrive at the comet in 2011, and during its eight-year journey, the spacecraft would pass by two asteroids. However, the *Rosetta*

The *Rosetta* probe lander settles on the surface of Comet Wirtanen in this computer-generated illustration. The lander is planned to rendezvous with the comet in 2011.

Mission has been postponed until February/March of 2004. The spacecraft has two parts, an orbiter and a lander. The *Rosetta* orbiter will explore the region surrounding the comet nucleus and the nucleus itself for at least two years. The *Rosetta* orbiter will come in for a close-up view, beginning at 3.25 AU and coming as close as about 0.6 miles (1 km).

RoLand (the *Rosetta* lander) will set down on the surface for the ultimate close-up. It will take and analyze samples from the surface and beam the results back to waiting scientists.

The *Rosetta* Mission is the next step beyond the fast "reconnaissance" flyby's done at Comet Halley, followed by the more thorough visits to Comet Grigg-Skjellerup (done in 1992 by *Giotto*) and to Comet Borrelly (made in 2001 by NASA's *Deep Space 1*).

Crater News: *Deep Impact*

What is a comet like deep inside? That's the question asked by investigators planning NASA's *Deep Impact* Mission, as they make ready for launch on December 30, 2004. The spacecraft will have two parts—a flyby spacecraft and a smaller "impactor." The two-part *Deep Impact* spacecraft is planned to arrive at Comet Tempel 1 in July 2005. Then the *Deep Impact* flyby spacecraft will point high-precision tracking telescopes at the comet and release the impactor, a large copper projectile. The purpose of the impactor is to hit the sunlit side of the comet with enough force to create a crater as wide as a football field and several stories deep.

Investigators hope to find out a lot about the interior of the comet by observing how the crater forms and how deep and wide it is. They will study the composition of the crater floor and its *ejecta* (the material thrown up and out of the crater). They will also note any changes in the gases naturally given off by the comet as a result of the impact. A camera flying on the impactor will capture images and relay them just before impact—possibly providing the best close-ups yet of a comet nucleus.

Meanwhile, the flyby portion of the spacecraft will collect data as it maneuvers within 300 miles (500 km) of the comet, fly through the coma, and then turn to observe the other side of the comet nucleus.

The Comet Tour: *CONTOUR*

The *Comet Nucleus Tour* (*CONTOUR*) was launched on July 3, 2002. The timing should have been just right for the space-craft to meet up with at least two comets as they arrived to visit the inner solar system—Comet Encke on November 12, 2003, and Comet Schwassmann-Wachmann 3 on June 18, 2006. But it was not to be. Contact with the spacecraft was lost on August 15, 2002, and attempts to regain it have failed.

Continuing Sagas

Perhaps in some ways the ancients were right. Comets are information carriers. But the information they carry is not the stuff of superstition, warnings, or omens. The information comets bring is much more important. With the help of science, comets today can tell us much about the history and structure of the solar system. Streaking across the nighttime skies, these exciting visitors, like the traveling storytellers of the past, continue to delight and inform us with their fascinating tales.

1059 B.C.E.	(Approximate) First recorded observation of a comet, in China.
1682 C.E.	Halley's Comet: Edmond Halley predicts the return of this comet.
1758	Halley's Comet returns, just as Halley predicted.
1950	Dutch astronomer Jan Hendrick Oort proposes that long-period comets come from a spherical shell of comet-related material that forms a cloud located at the outer edge of the solar system.
1985	*ISEE-3/ICE* flies by Comet Giacobini-Zinner and becomes the first spacecraft to fly by a comet.
1986	Multiple spacecraft fly by Comet Halley: *ICE*, USSR's *Vega 1* and *Vega 2*, ESA's *Giotto*, and Japan's *Sakigake* and *Suisei*.
1992	*Giotto* flies by Comet Grigg-Skjellerup. *Ulysses* also becomes part of a Comet Watch Program on its way to the Sun.

1993	Astronomers realize the Comet Shoemaker-Levy 9 is going to smash into Jupiter.
1994	Shoemaker-Levy 9, broken into pieces by Jupiter's gravitational force, collides into Jupiter in July.
1996	*ROSAT* orbiting X-ray telescope detects X rays in a comet for the first time—in Comet Hyakutake.
1998	*Deep Space 1* is launched to test an ion propulsion system; later flies by Comet Borrelly in 2001.
1999	Launch of *Stardust*, first dedicated comet flyby mission since *Giotto*.
2001	*Deep Space 1* flies by Comet Borrelly.
2002	*Comet Nucleus Tour (CONTOUR)* launched in July for a comet flyby mission at Comet Encke and Comet Schwassmann-Wachmann 3. Loss of signal in August ends the mission.
2004	Planned. Launch of *Rosetta*, a European comet lander/orbiter mission to Comet Wirtanen.

2004	—	Planned. *STARDUST* encounter with Comet Wild-2. Launch of *Deep Impact*, a comet impact/ flyby mission to Comet Tempel 1.
2005	—	Planned. *Deep Impact* to arrive at Comet Tempel 1.
2006	—	Planned. *STARDUST* to drop off a sample return of comet dust to Earth.
2011	—	Planned. *Rosetta* to arrive at Comet Wirtanen for lander/orbiter mission.
2014	—	Planned. Return of *ICE* to Earth.

accretion—the process of accumulation of matter into objects such as comets, asteroids, planets, and stars

active comet—a comet that has begun to sublimate ice and form a coma due to the Sun's heat. (See *coma*.)

asteroid—a large—greater than 0.6 miles (1 km)—leftover chunk of material not included in any planet during formation; also, part of a planet broken off by a collision. (See *meteoroid*.)

asteroid belt—region between Mars and Jupiter, where most asteroids orbit

atmosphere—gases surrounding a planet or moon

astrology—the nonscientific attempt to predict supposed effects of positions and movements of the planets and stars on human lives and events on Earth

astronomical unit (AU)—a unit of measurement equal to the mean distance from Earth to the Sun, a distance of 93 million miles (150 million km.)

astronomy—the scientific study of the universe—including the position, composition, dynamics, and history of planets, comets, asteroids, and stars

CCD—"charge-coupled device," the array of photosensitive detectors that, when read by a microprocessor, provide photographic images; a CCD can detect even the smallest unit of light, a photon.

coma—a sphere-shaped envelope of gas and dust that develops around a comet when it becomes active. (See *active comet*.)

comet—a solar system object that has a solid nucleus and in most cases is surrounded by an enormous coma up to 1.5 million miles (2.4 million km) in diameter and a vapor tail during the portions of its orbit that are closest to the Sun

cometary nucleus—the solid part of a comet, usually about the size of a city in diameter, composed of ices and dust grains

cometary trail—vast collection of large dust particles and debris following a comet's orbit

composition—what something, such as a comet or moon, is made of

core—the distinct region that is located at the center of a planet or moon; most small bodies (such as comets) have the same composition throughout and are not said to have a core

crater—a rimmed basin or depression in the surface of a planet or moon, caused by the impact of a meteoroid or asteroid

crust—the outer solid surface layer of an object, such as a meteoroid, asteroid, planet, or moon

density—how much of a substance exists in a given volume, usually measured in grams per cubic centimeter

diameter—the distance across the center of a circle or sphere

eccentric—describes the extent to which a curve varies from a closed, perfectly round circle. An ellipse is more eccentric than a circle because even though it is closed it is flattened, not perfectly round. A parabola is even more eccentric; it is not closed—that is, its curved arms never meet. All cometary orbits are eccentric (as are all planetary orbits).

ejecta—material thrown up and out of a crater on impact

elliptical—oval-shaped; most orbits are elliptical

gravity—A force of attraction between two objects having mass, such as a planet or moon; the attraction exerted by an object with mass

highly eccentric—describes an elliptical orbit that is much longer than it is wide, that is, very flattened

interplanetary—between the planets

ion—an atom that has an electrical charge because it has gained or lost one or more electrons

jets—irregular streams of gases sublimed by the Sun's heat from a comet's nuclear ices, carrying dust away with them from the surface

Kuiper belt—sometimes called the Edgeworth-Kuiper belt, the region beyond Pluto and Neptune, where a group of planetoids orbit the Sun; an area that may supply many short-period comets

magnetosphere—the region around a planet in which the planet's magnetic field affects the flow of the changed particles of the solar wind. The magnetic field essentially deflects the particles so they flow around the planet rather than to it.

mass—the amount of material a body contains, usually measured in grams

meteor—a bright streak of light high in the sky caused by passage of a space rock through Earth's atmosphere, a "shooting star"

meteor shower—a group of "shooting stars," or meteors, the visible entry into Earth's atmosphere of small fragments of a comet or meteoroid *meteorite*—a chunk of a rock from space that has struck the surface of a planet or moon

meteoroid—a small—up to about 0.6 miles (1 km across)—chunk of material not included in any planet during formation; also, part of a planet broken off by a collision. (See *asteroid*.)

orbit—the path traveled by an object as it revolves around another body

perturb—to cause a variation in the orbit of a meteoroid or other object; usually caused by another object's gravity

planetesimals—leftover gas and ash from the formation of the Sun that clumped together to become the planets and moons of the solar system

plasma—a gaslike substance composed of nearly equal amounts of positively charged ions and electrons (negatively charged ions)— and therefore almost neutral in electrical charge

radiant point—a point in the sky from which meteors in a meteor shower seem to be falling; an illusion of perspective

revolve—to move in a path, or orbit, around another object. The Earth revolves around the Sun, making a complete trip, or revolution, in one year.

rotate—to turn on its axis.

solar nebula—a primitive cloud of gas and dust from which the Sun, planets, comets, and asteroids were born

solar wind—a stream of charged particles that flows at high speeds from the Sun's surface

tidal force—the difference in the force of gravity exerted on the near and far sides of an object; for example, the giant planet Jupiter exerts considerable tidal forces on objects that pass nearby, such as the Comet Shoemaker-Levy 9

The news from space changes fast, so it's always a good idea to check the copyright date on books, CD-ROMs, and video tapes to make sure that you are getting up-to-date information. One good place to look for current information from NASA is U.S. government depository libraries. There are several in each state.

Books

Campbell, Ann Jeanette. *The New York Public Library Amazing Space: A Book of Answers for Kids.* New York: John Wiley & Sons, 1997.

Sagan, Carl, and Ann Druyan. *Comet,* revised edition. New York: Ballantine Books, 1995.

Sparrow, Giles. *Asteroids, Comets, & Meteors* (Exploring the Solar System). Chicago: Heinemann Library, 2001.

Vogt, Gregory. *Asteroids, Comets, and Meteors.* Austin, Tx: Steadwell Books, 2001.

Vogt, Gregory L. *The Solar System: Facts and Exploration.* Scientific American Sourcebooks. New York: Twenty-First Century Books, 1995.

Videotapes

Cosmic Travelers: Comets and Asteroids (The Cosmic Travelers Series), 1998.

This videotape explores the likelihood of collisions between Earth and the "cosmic travelers," comets and asteroids. It includes accounts of past collisions and plans for preventing big collisions in the future, illustrated with deep-space photos, as well as 3-D animation and computer graphics. The series includes two other related videos: Goldhil Home Media. VHS format.

Comets and Asteroids (Just the Facts Learning Series), 1997.

Interviews with comet and asteroid researchers provide insights into these small interplanetary bodies. Computer graphics, photos of comets, and footage on impact craters help provide an exploration of what scientists know about comets and asteroids—and their effects on Earth's ecology. Goldhil Home Media. VHS format.

Magazine

Discover Magazine: Solar System
Discovery Channel School
P.O. Box 970
Oxon Hill, MD 20750-0970

Organizations and Online Sites

Many of the online sites listed below are NASA sites, with links to many other interesting sources of information about comets and the other objects of the solar system. You can also sign up to receive NASA news on many subjects via e-mail.

The Antarctic Search for Meteorites (ANSMET)
http://www.cwru.edu/affil/ansmet/index.html
Answers frequently asked questions, providing background and information about the search for meteorites in Antarctica—some of which are small chunks of comets with Earth-crossing orbits.

Asteroid and Comet Collisions
http://www.spaceref.com/Directory/Astronomy/Asteroids_And_Comets/
Provides a page of links to organizations that maintain a skywatch for Earth-crossing asteroids and comets.

Astronomical Society of the Pacific
390 Ashton Avenue
San Francisco, CA 94112
http://www.astrosociety.org/

Meteorite and Impact Advisory Committee to the Canadian Space Agency

http://wwwdsa.uqac.uquebec.ca/~mhiggins/MIAC/MIAC.html
Provides information about Canadian finds and falls, craters and cratering, including photos, drawings, and information about types of meteorites and examples.

NASA Ask a Space Scientist

http://image.gsfc.nasa.gov/poetry/ask/askmag.html#list
Interactive page where NASA scientists answer your questions about astronomy, space, and space missions. Also offers archives and fact sheets

The Nine Planets: A Multimedia Tour of the Solar System

http://www.seds.org/nineplanets/nineplanets/nineplanets.html
Includes excellent material on solar system objects, including comets, from the Students for the Exploration and Development of Space, University of Arizona.

Sky Online

http://www.skypub.com
The Web site for *Sky and Telescope* magazine and other publications of Sky Publishing Corporation. This site has a good weekly news section on general space and astronomy news. The site also contains many good tips for amateur astronomers, as well as a nice selection of links. A list of

science museums, planetariums, and astronomy clubs organized by state helps locate nearby places to visit, as well.

Places to Visit

Check the Internet (*www.skypub.com* is a good place to start), your local visitor's center, or phone directory for planetariums and science museums near you. Here are a few other suggestions:

Exploratorium
3601 Lyon Street
San Francisco, CA 94123
http://www.exploratorium.edu/
Internationally acclaimed interactive science exhibits, including astronomy subjects.

Jet Propulsion Laboratory (JPL)
4800 Oak Grove Drive
Pasadena, CA 91109
http://www.jpl.nasa.gov/
Tours available once or twice a week by arrangement; see Web site for instructions, or telephone or write to the JPL visitor contact. JPL is the primary mission center for most NASA solar system missions.

Index

Bold numbers indicate illustrations.

Ray Spangenburg and **Kit Moser** are a husband-and-wife writing team specializing in science and technology. They have written over 50 books and more than 100 articles, including a five-book series on the history of science and a four-book series on the history of space exploration. As journalists, they have covered NASA and related science activities for many years. They have flown on NASA's Kuiper Airborne Observatory, covered stories at the Deep Space Network in the Mojave Desert, and experienced zero gravity on experimental NASA flights out of NASA's Ames Research Center. They live in Carmichael, California, with their Boston terrier, F. Scott Fitz.